CONTEMPO...
MUSICAL THEATRE F...

YOUNG WOMEN'S EDITION VOLUME 1

31 SONGS FROM 25 MUSICALS

ISBN 978-1-4803-9518-3

HAL•LEONARD®
CORPORATION
7777 W. BLUEMOUND RD. P.O. BOX 13819 MILWAUKEE, WI 53213

Visit Hal Leonard Online at
www.halleonard.com

CONTENTS

PULLED
from *The Addams Family*

Music and Lyrics by
Andrew Lippa

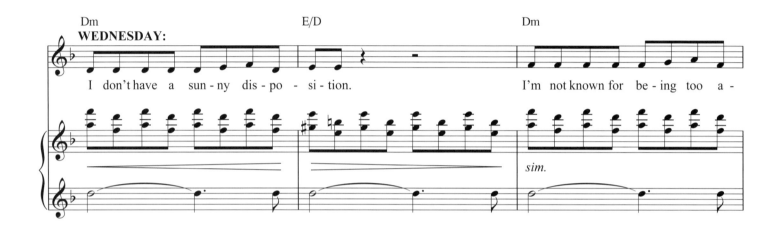

WEDNESDAY:
I don't have a sun-ny dis-po-si-tion. I'm not known for be-ing too a-

mused. My de-mean-or's locked in one po-si-tion. See my

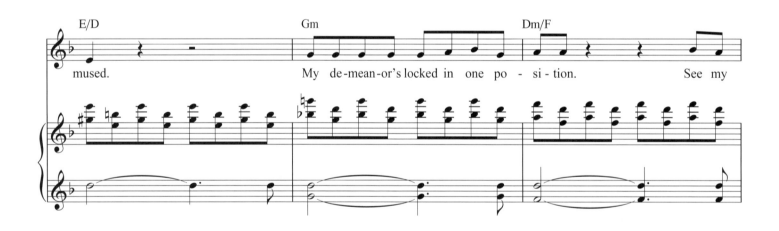

face? I'm en-thused. Sud-den-ly, how-ev-er, I've been

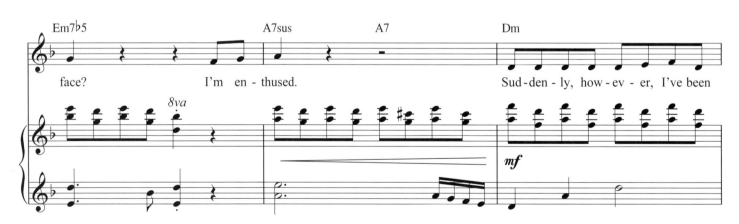

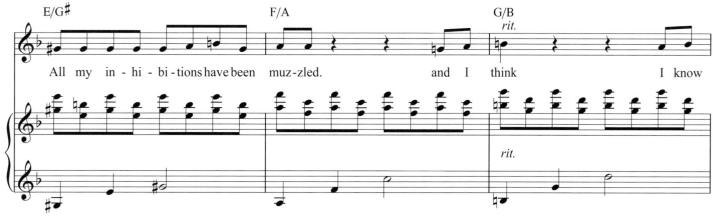

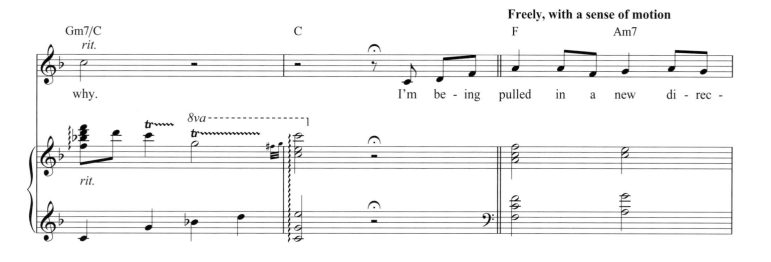

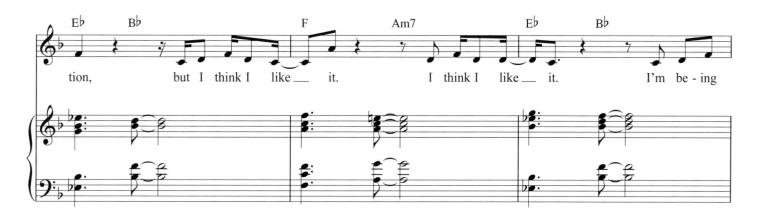

pulled in a new di-rec-tion. Through my pain-ful pur-suit ___ some-how

bird-ies took root. ___ All the things I de-test - ed im-pos - si-bly cute. ___ God!

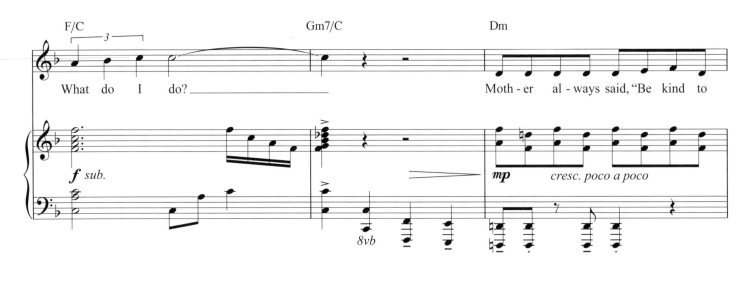

What do I do? _____ Moth-er al-ways said, "Be kind to

stran gers." But she does-n't know what they de - stroy.

I can feel the clear and pres-ent dan-gers when she learns that the

boy _____ has got me pulled in a new di-rec-

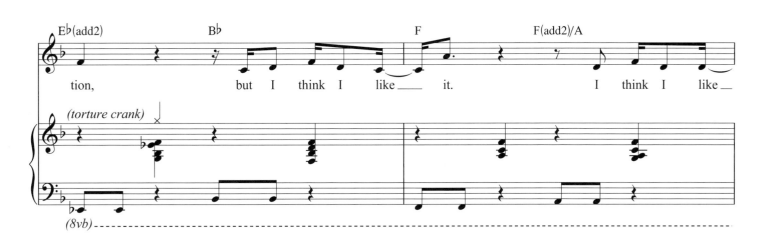

tion, but I think I like ____ it. I think I like ____

____ it. I'm be-ing pulled in a new di-rec-tion. And this

EASY AS LIFE
from Elton John and Tim Rice's *Aida*

Music by Elton John
Lyrics by Tim Rice

Pas - sion would have cooled and all the mag - ic would have died.

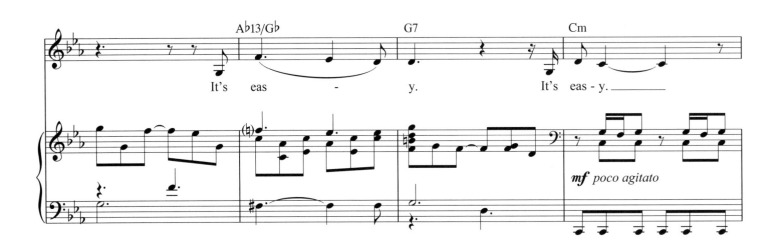

It's eas - y. It's eas - y.

mf poco agitato

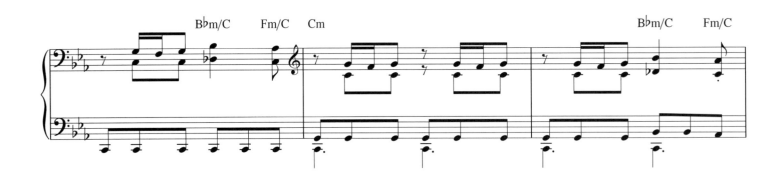

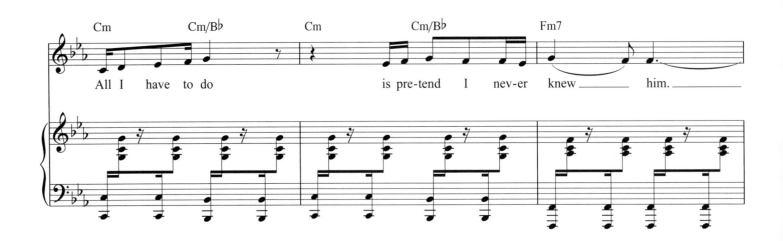

All I have to do is pre-tend I nev-er knew him.

MIX TAPE
from the Broadway Musical *Avenue Q*

Music and Lyrics by Robert Lopez
and Jeff Marx

He likes me. I think he

likes me. But does he like - me - like - me,

like I like him? Will we be

Avenue Q has not been authorized or approved in any manner by The Jim Henson Company or Sesame Workshop which have no responsibility for its content.

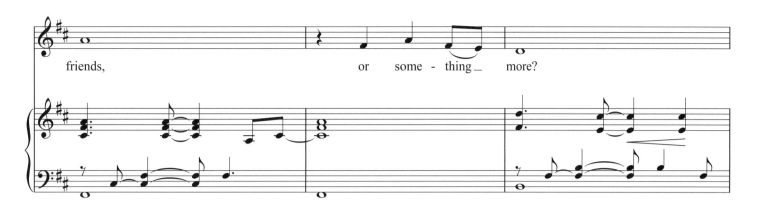

friends,　　　　　or　some - thing　more?

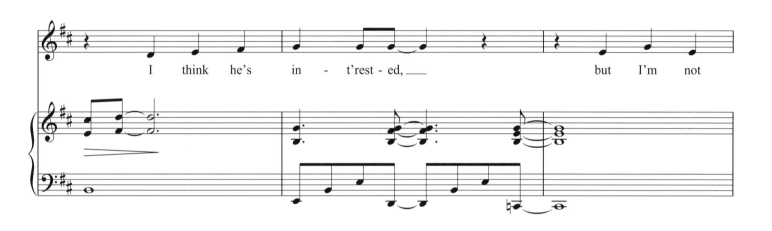

I　think　he's　in - t'rest - ed, ___　　　but　I'm　not

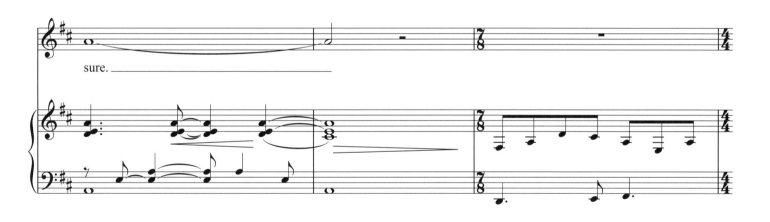

sure. _____

A

mix tape. He made a mix tape.

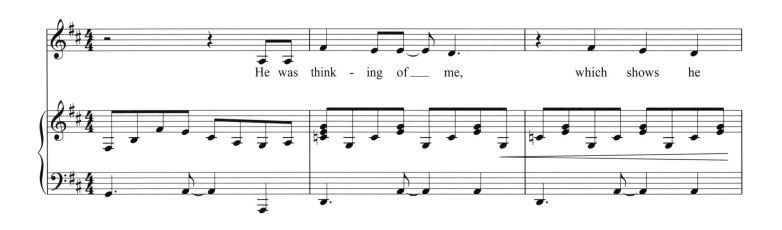

He was think - ing of __ me, which shows he

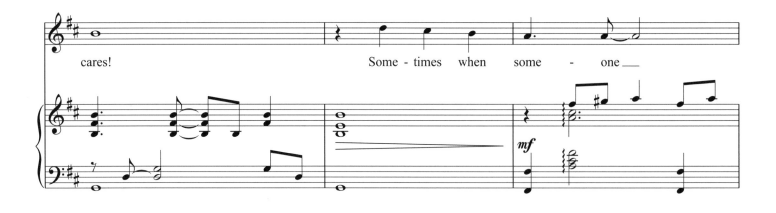

cares! Some - times when some - one __

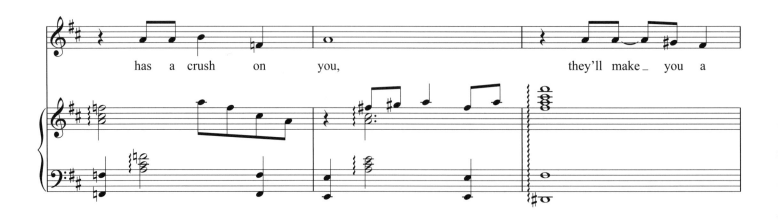

has a crush on you, they'll make _ you a

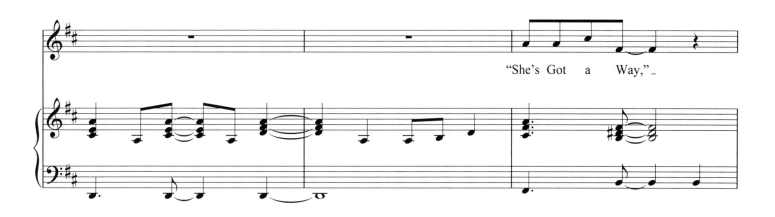

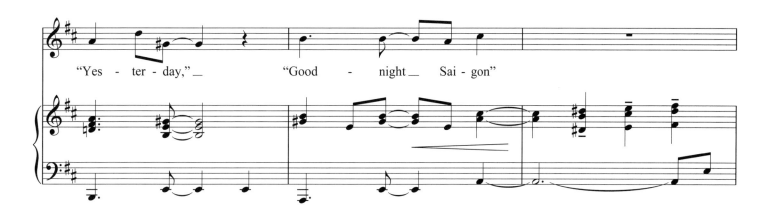

"Through the Years," ___ "The

Theme from 'Cheers'," ___ "Mov-ing Right A-long." ___ *Nice tape. Oh, but there's one more...* "I

Have to Say ___ I Love ___ You in ___ a Song." _____

He likes me.

THERE'S A FINE, FINE LINE

from the Broadway Musical *Avenue Q*

Music and Lyrics by Robert Lopez
and Jeff Marx

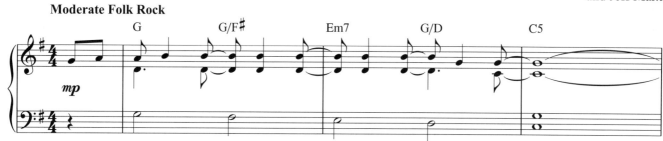

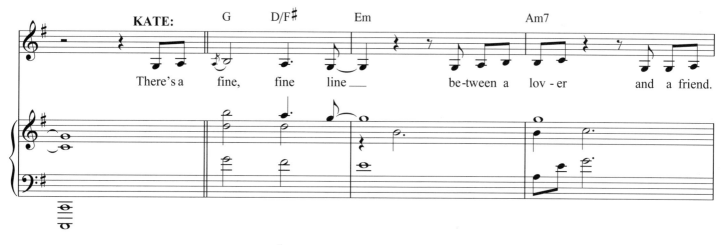

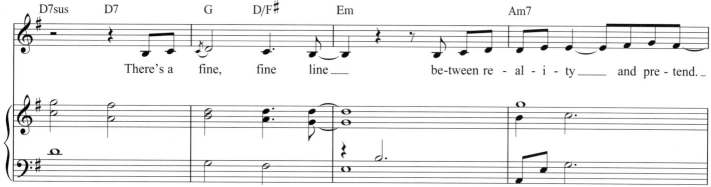

KILLER INSTINCT
from *Bring It On*

Music by Tom Kitt
Lyrics by Amanda Green

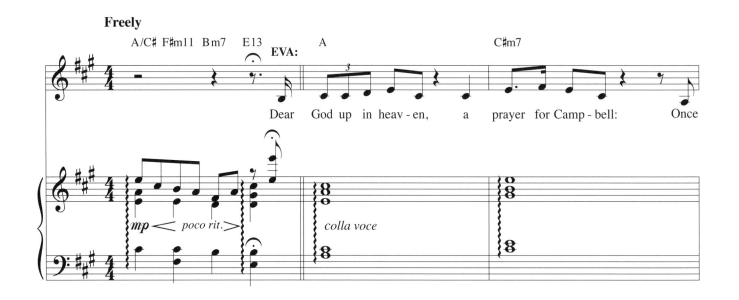

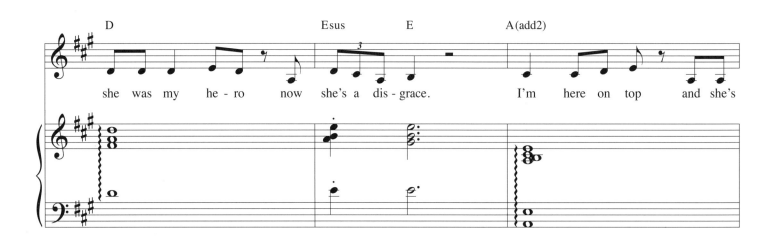

ONE PERFECT MOMENT

from *Bring It On*

Music by Tom Kitt
Lyrics by Amanda Green
and Lin-Manuel Miranda

Freely, but with slight urgency

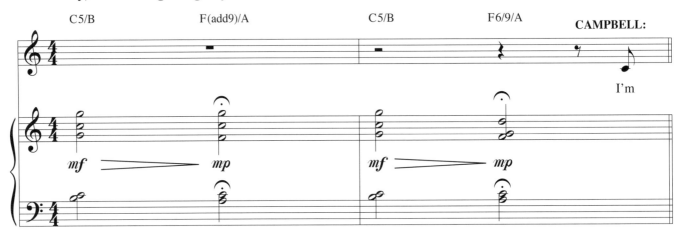

CAMPBELL:

I'm

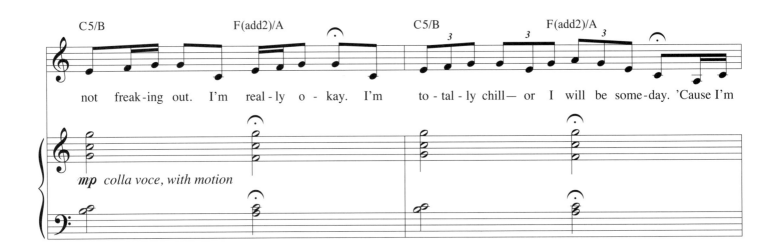

not freak-ing out. I'm real-ly o-kay. I'm to-tal-ly chill— or I will be some-day. 'Cause I'm

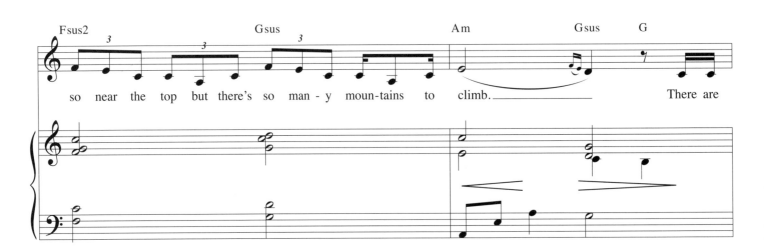

so near the top but there's so man-y moun-tains to climb. There are

48

BRIDE'S LAMENT

from *The Drowsy Chaperone*

Words and Music by Lisa Lambert
and Greg Morrison

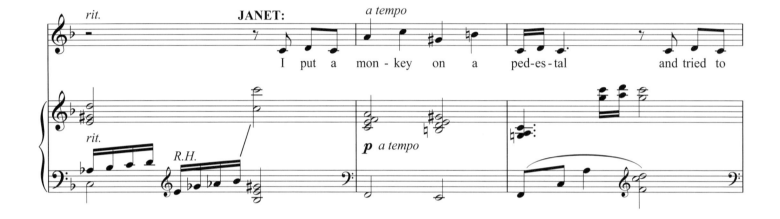

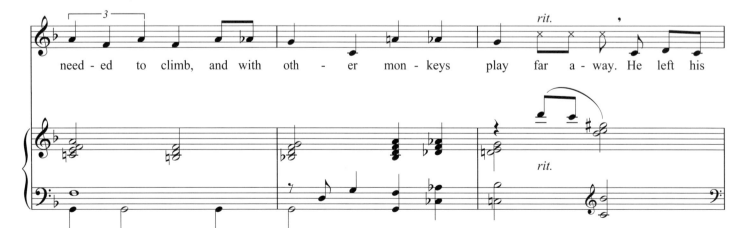

Janet is joined by Man in Chair and chorus in the show, adapted here as a solo.

Faster, in 4

Ger-trude Stein, she hand-ed me a rose. I'm

Jan - et, Jan - et Van De Graaff. Ain't no nail that

I can't ham - mer. Why give up a life of glam - or,

(she's having a complete mental breakdown)

life of glam - or, life of glam - or? No!

mon - key gone a - stray. I ask the

stars a - bove: is it the mon - key or my

ped - es - tal I love?

I CAN HEAR THE BELLS
from *Hairspray*

Music by Marc Shaiman
Lyrics by Marc Shaiman and Scott Wittman

* Optional ending

I WON'T SAY
(I'm in Love)
from Walt Disney Pictures' *Hercules*

Music by Alan Menken
Lyrics by David Zippel

-ey, they can see right through you. Girl, ya can't con-ceal it, they __ know how ya feel and who you're

think - ing of. __ Oh. __ No chance, no way, __

__ I won't say __ it, no, no. You swoon, __ you sigh, __ why de - ny __ it, uh oh. __

__ It's too __ cli - ché, __ I won't say __ I'm in love.

STILL HURTING

from *The Last Five Years*

Music and Lyrics by
Jason Robert Brown

WHAT I'VE BEEN LOOKING FOR
from the Disney Channel Original Movie *High School Musical*

Words and Music by Andy Dodd
and Adam Watts

It's hard to be - lieve ___ that I could-n't see ___ you were

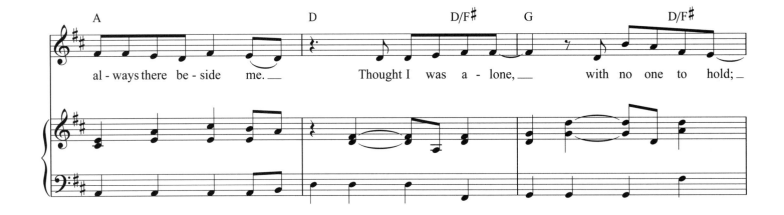

al - ways there be - side me. ___ Thought I was a - lone, ___ with no one to hold; ___

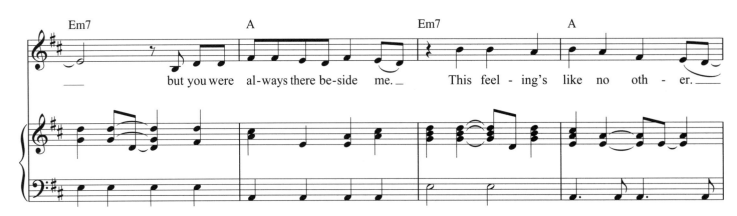

___ but you were al - ways there be-side me. ___ This feel - ing's like no oth - er. ___

Originally a duet, this song has been adapted for this solo edition.

I've been look-ing for. _____

So good to be seen; __ so good to be heard. _____ Don't

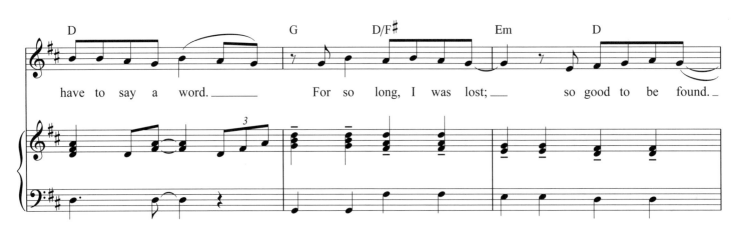

have to say a word. _____ For so long, I was lost; __ so good to be found. _

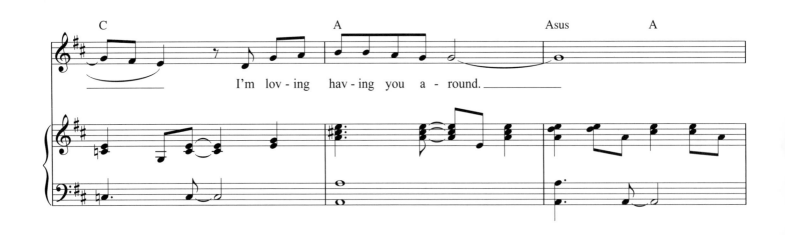

_____ I'm lov-ing hav-ing you a-round. _____

IRELAND
from *Legally Blonde*

Music and Lyrics by Laurence O'Keefe
and Nell Benjamin

PAULETTE: *Elle, do you know the number one
reason behind all bad hair decisions?*

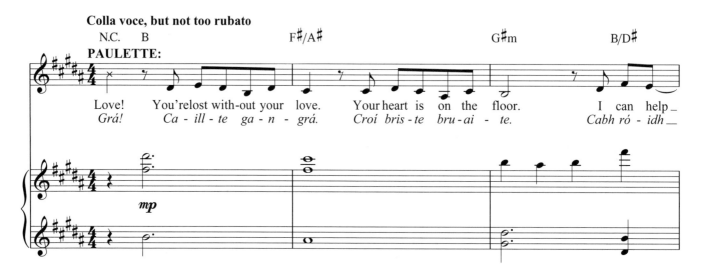

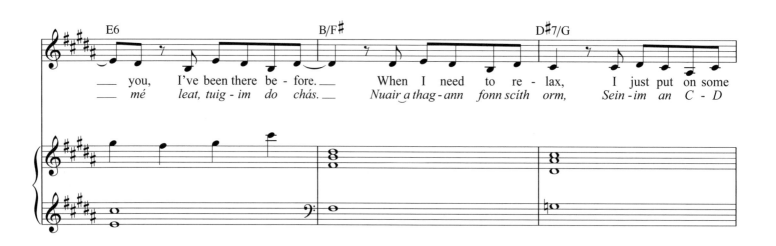

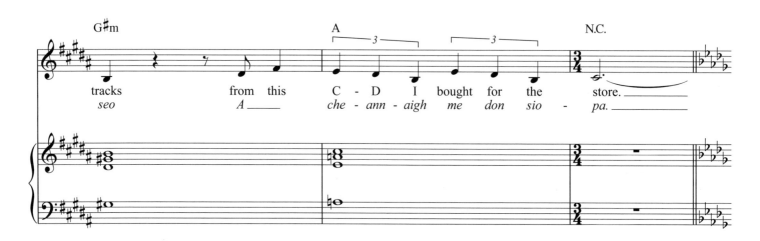

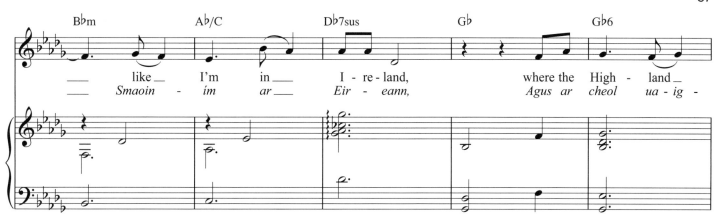

like __ I'm in __ I - re - land, where the High - land __
_Smaoin - ím ar __ Eir - eann, Agus ar cheol ua - ig -_

A little faster

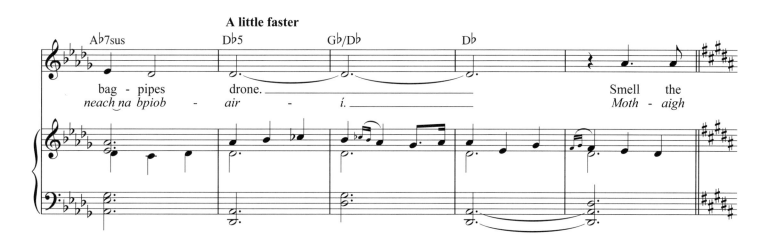

bag - pipes drone. __ Smell the
_neach na bpiob - air - í. __ Moth - aigh_

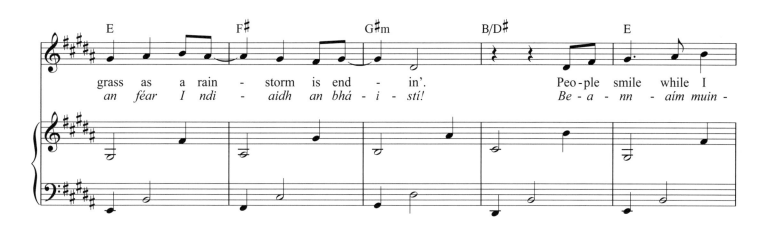

grass as a rain - storm is end - in'. Peo - ple smile while I
an féar I ndi - aidh an bhá - i - stí! Be - a - nn - aím muin -

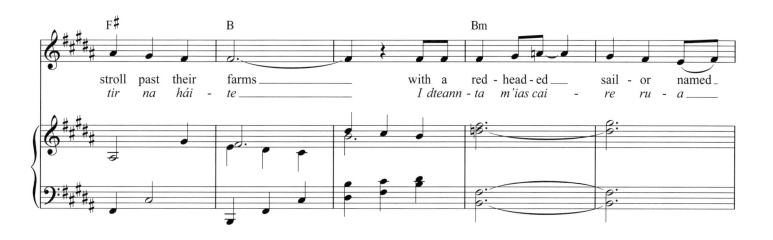

stroll past their farms __ with a red - head - ed __ sail - or named __
_tir na hái - te __ I dteann - ta m'ias cai - re ru - a ___

THE BEAUTY IS
from *The Light in the Piazza*

Words and Music by
Adam Guettel

4/10

With a strong pulse

CLARA:

These   are ver - y   pop - u - lar   in   It - a - ly!

in It - a - ly. Ev - ery-one's a fa - ther or

a son.___ I think if I had a child___

I would take such care of her.___ Then I would - n't

feel like one._____ I've

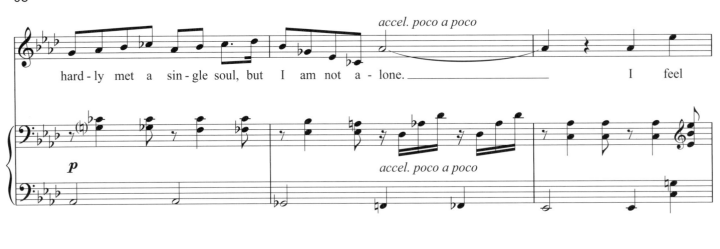

accel. poco a poco

hard-ly met a sin-gle soul, but I am not a-lone._____ I feel

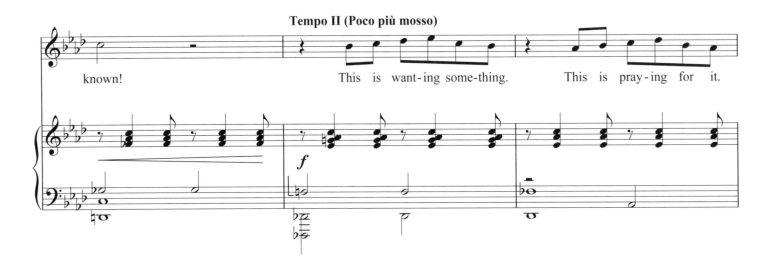

Tempo II (Poco più mosso)

known!   This is want-ing some-thing.   This is pray-ing for it.

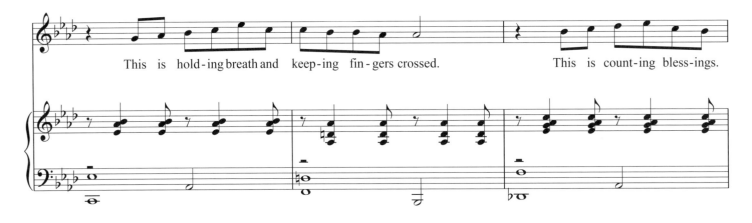

This is hold-ing breath and keep-ing fin-gers crossed.   This is count-ing bless-ings.

This is won-d'ring when   I'll see that__ boy a-gain.__

PART OF YOUR WORLD
from Walt Disney's *The Little Mermaid - A Broadway Musical*

Music by Alan Menken
Lyrics by Howard Ashman

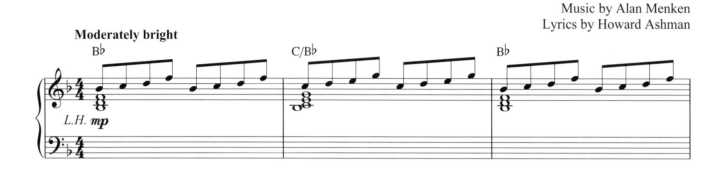

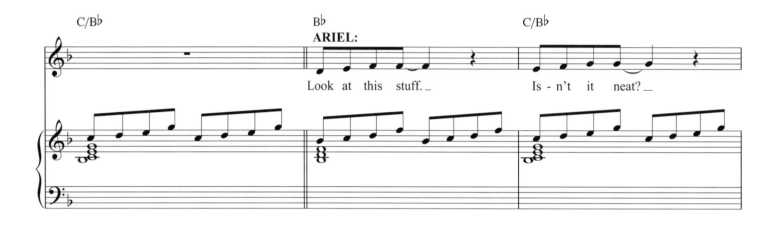

ARIEL:

Look at this stuff. _ Is - n't it neat? _

Would-n't you think _ my col - lec -tion's com - plete? Would-n't you think _ I'm the girl, _

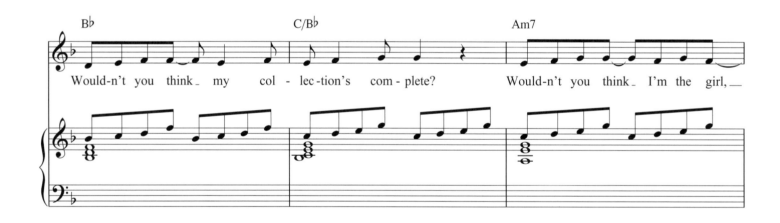

_ the girl who has ev - 'ry - thing. _

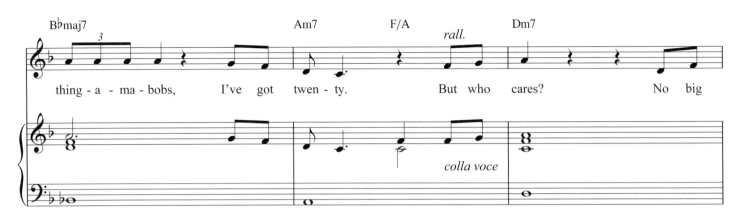

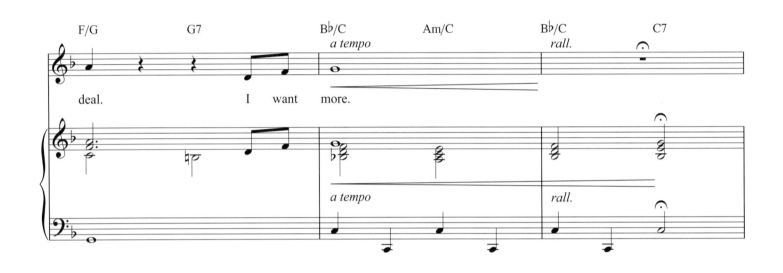

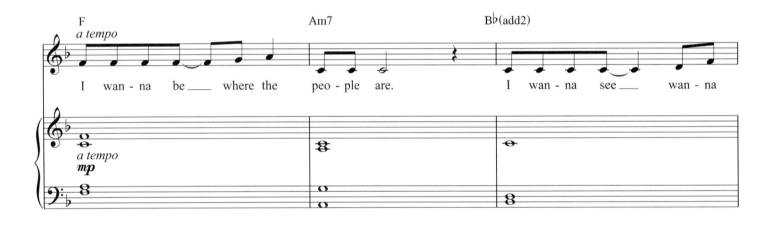

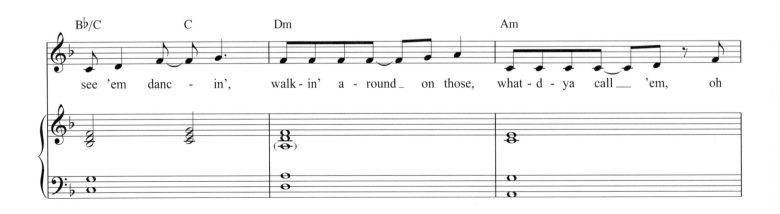

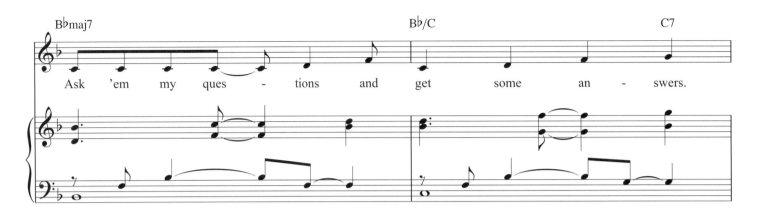

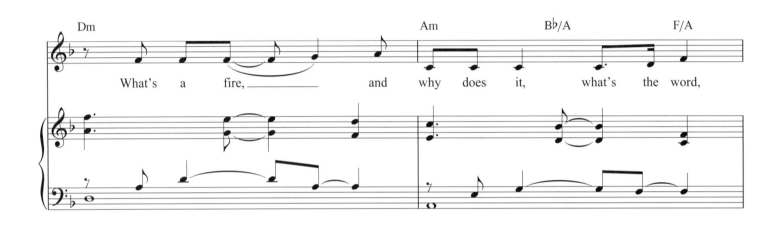

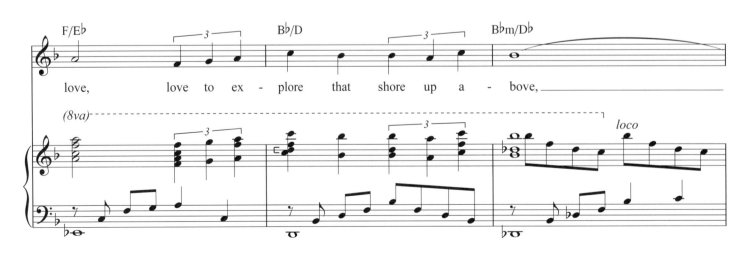

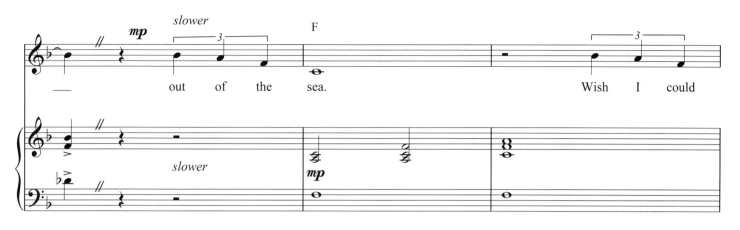

out of the sea. Wish I could

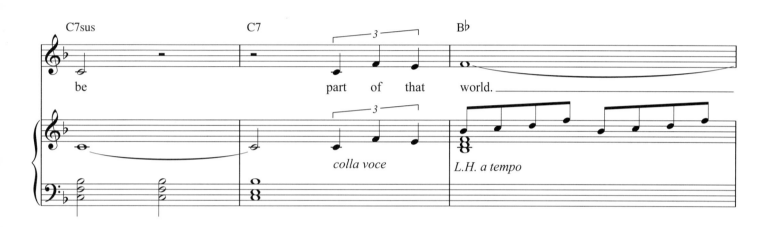

be part of that world.

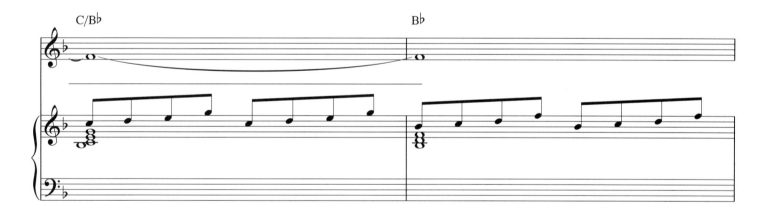

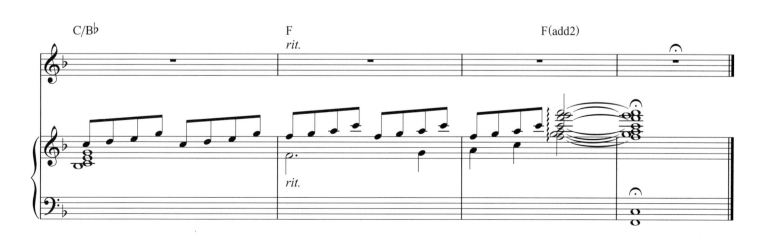

THE WORLD ABOVE

from Walt Disney's *The Little Mermaid - A Broadway Musical*

Music by Alan Menken
Lyrics by Glenn Slater

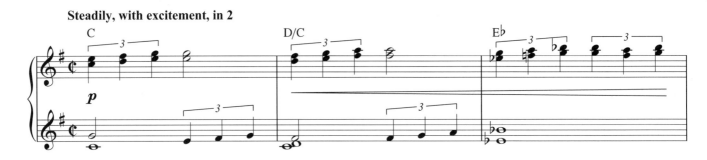

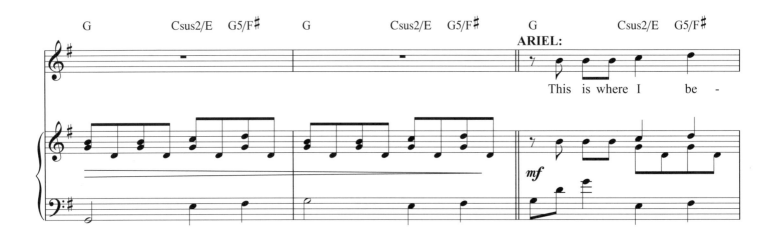

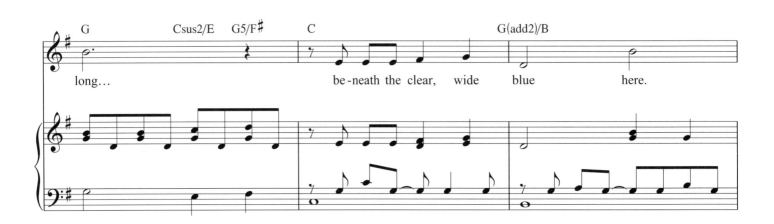

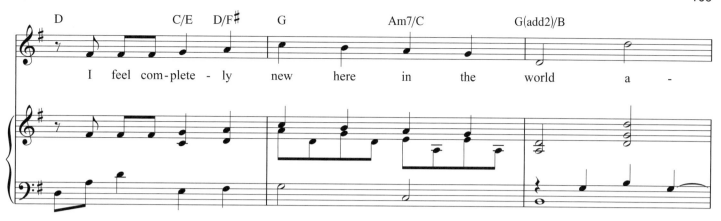

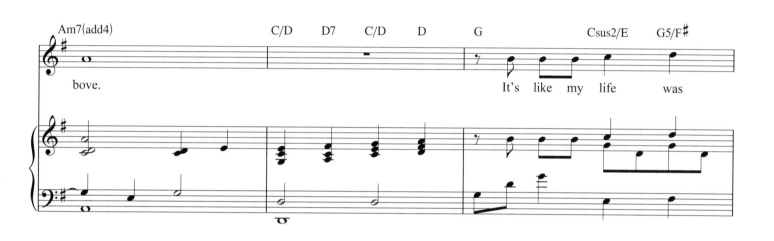

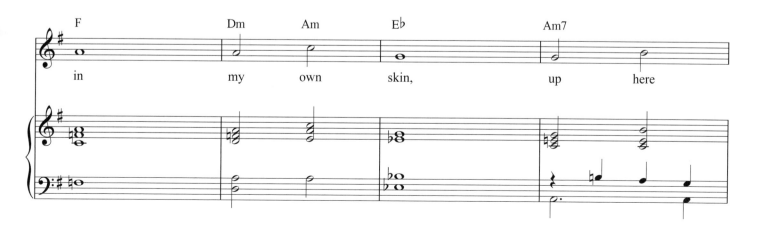

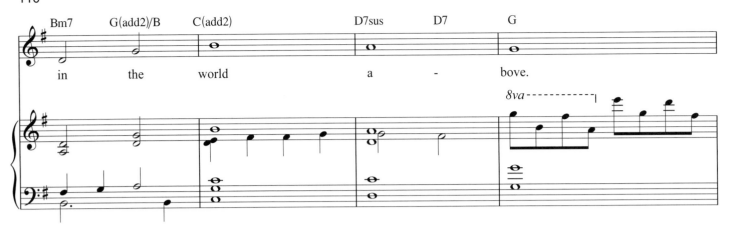

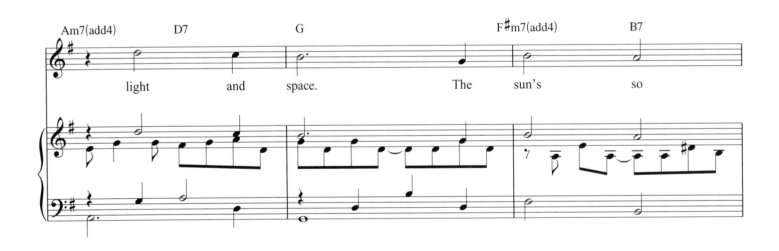

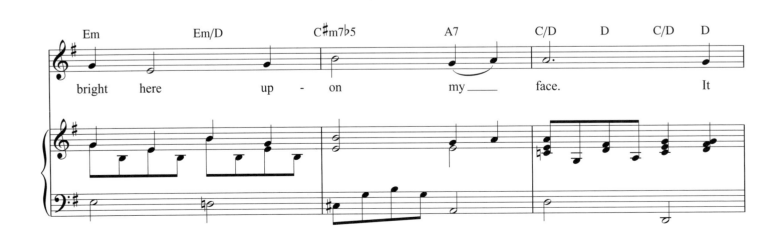

feels so right here, warm as

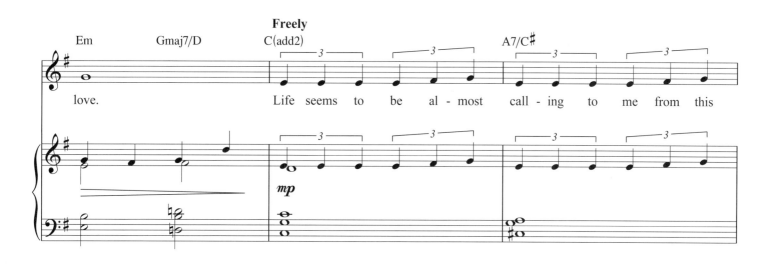

love. Life seems to be al - most call - ing to me from this

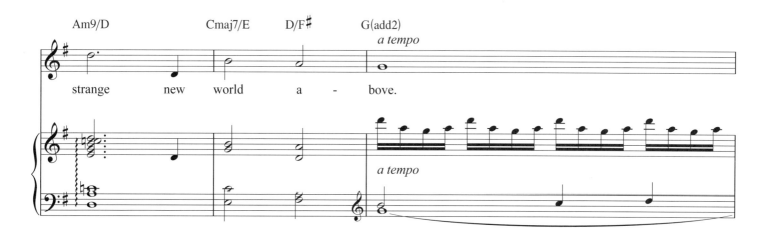

strange new world a - bove.

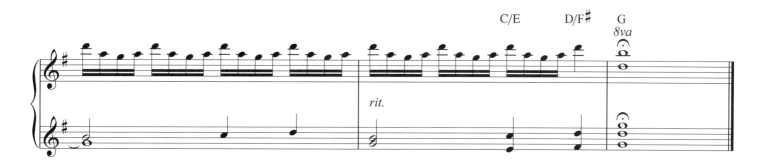

SOME THINGS ARE MEANT TO BE

from the Stage Musical *Little Women*

Music by Jason Howland
Lyrics by Mindi Dickstein

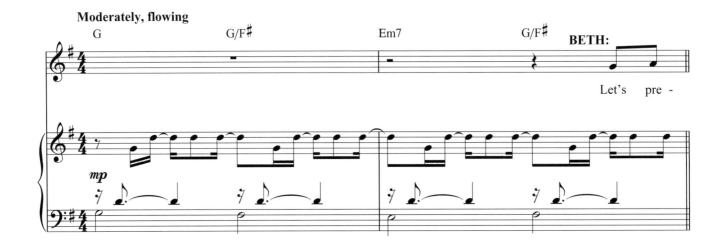

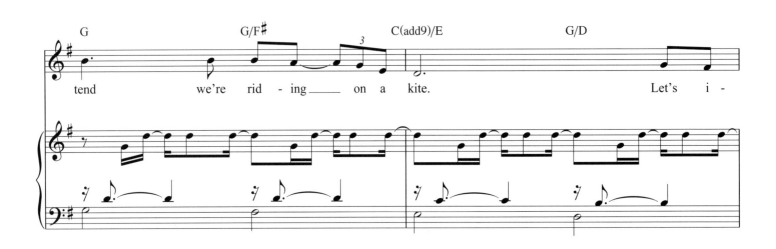

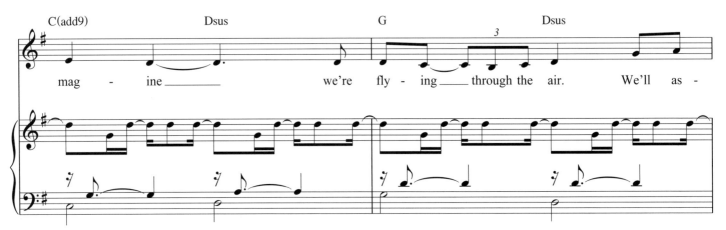

This duet for Beth and Jo is adapted as a solo.

118

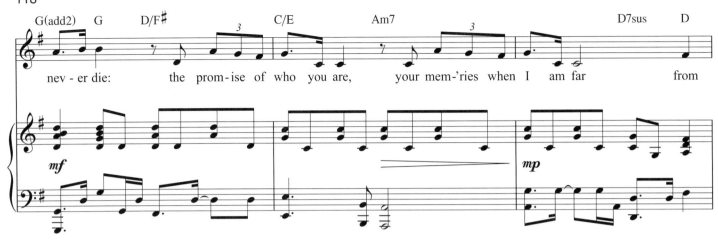

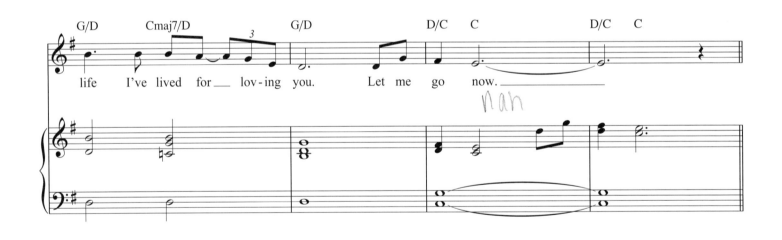

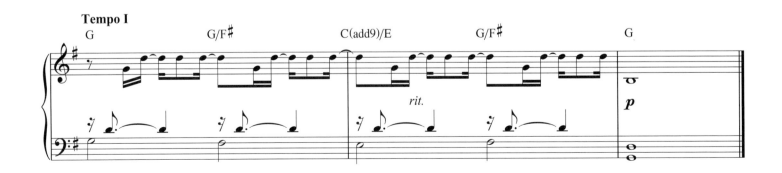

WHATEVER HAPPENED TO MY PART?

from *Monty Python's Spamalot*

Lyrics by Eric Idle
Music by John Du Prez and Eric Idle

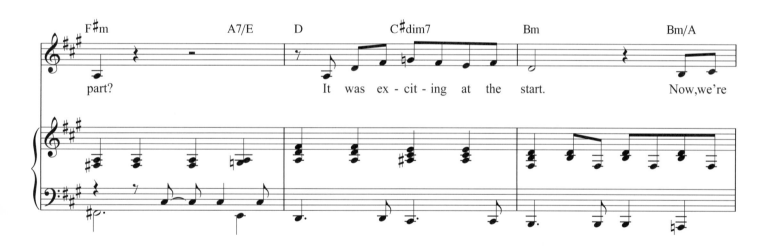

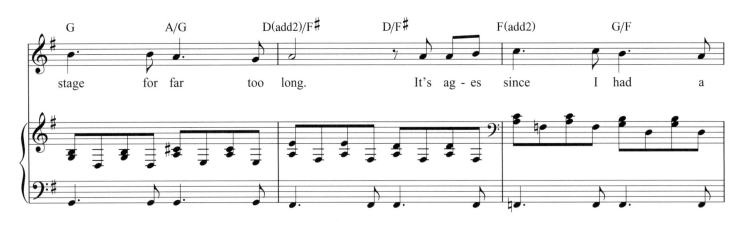

stage for far too long. It's ag - es since I had a

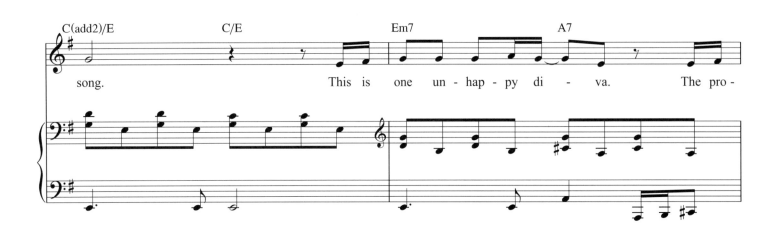

song. This is one un - hap - py di - va. The pro -

duc - ers have de - ceived her. There is noth - ing I can sing from my

heart. What - ev - er hap - pened to my part? I am

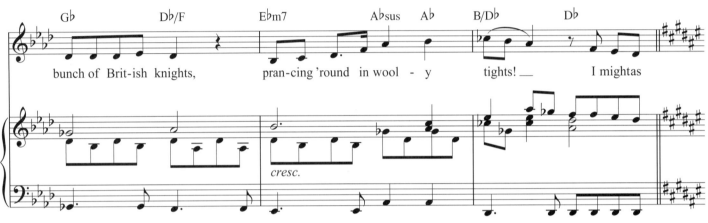

PRINCESS
from *A Man of No Importance*

Words by Lynn Ahrens
Music by Stephen Flaherty

Moderately fast folk ($\quad$ = 92)

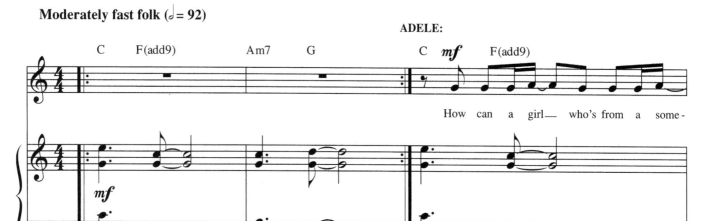

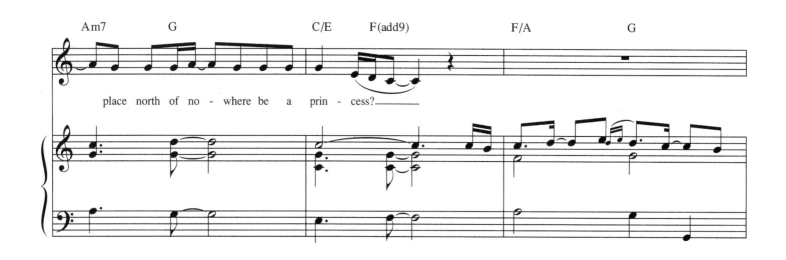

WATCH WHAT HAPPENS
from Walt Disney's *Newsies - The Musical*

Music by Alan Menken
Lyrics by Jack Feldman

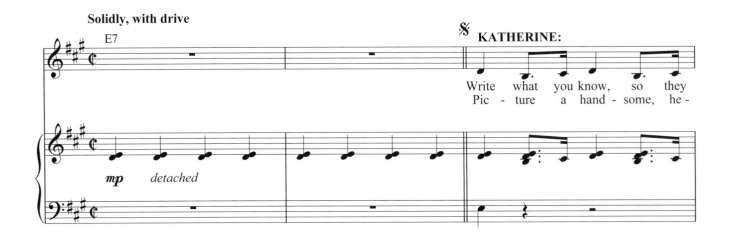

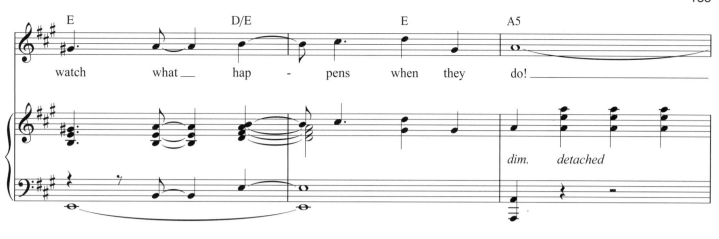

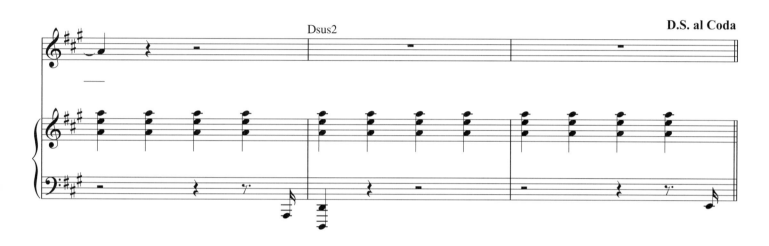

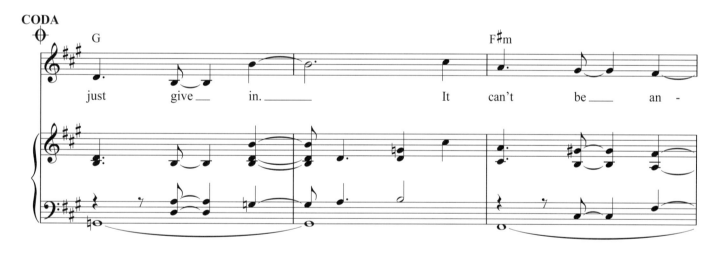

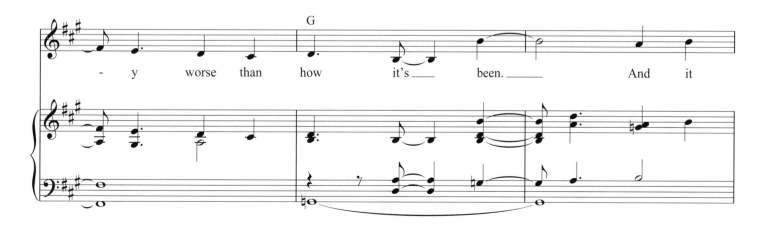

ALL FOR YOU
from *Seussical the Musical*

Words by Lynn Ahrens
Music by Stephen Flaherty

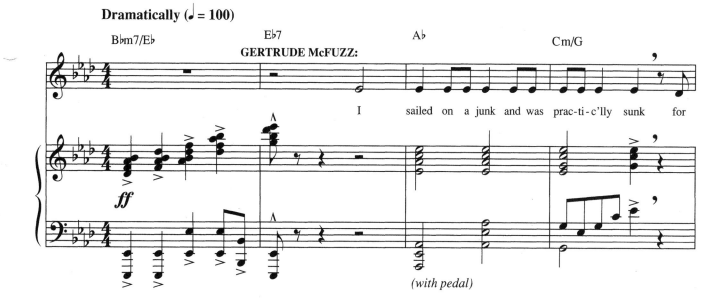

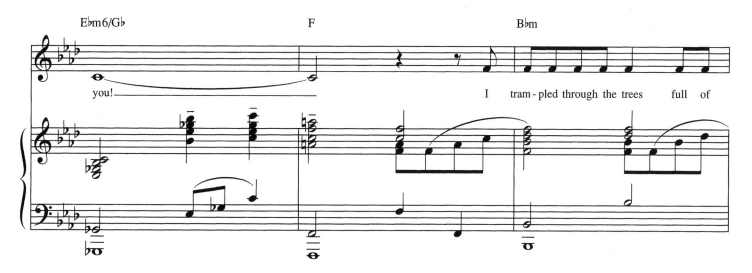

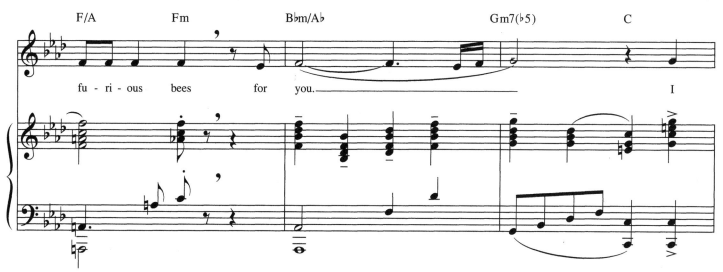

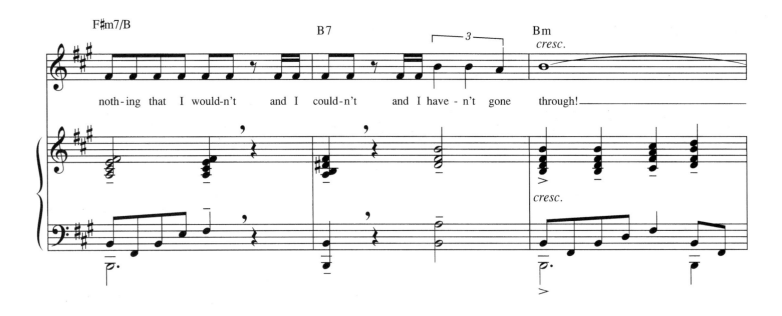

noth-ing that I would-n't and I could-n't and I have-n't gone through!

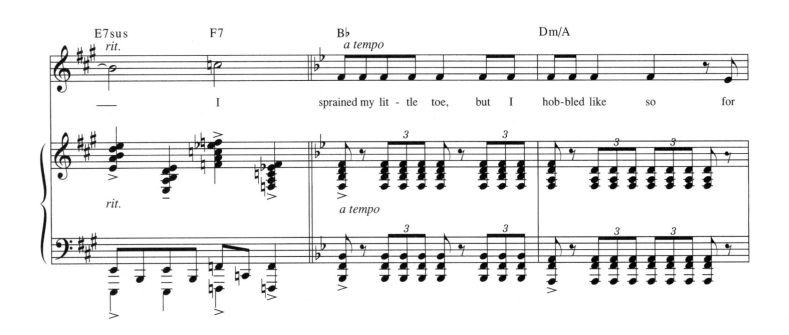

I sprained my lit-tle toe, but I hob-bled like so for

you. Then came the hit and run but I

WITHOUT YOU
from *Rent*

Words and Music by
Jonathan Larson

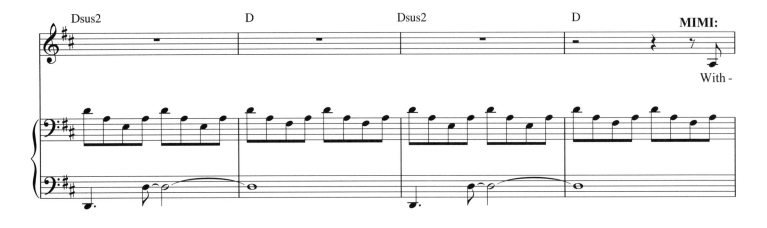

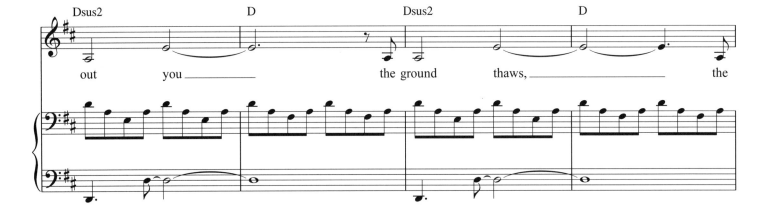

This song for Mimi and Roger has been adapted as a solo for this edition.

MORNING PERSON

from *Shrek the Musical*

Words and Music by Jeanine Tesori
and David Lindsay-Abaire

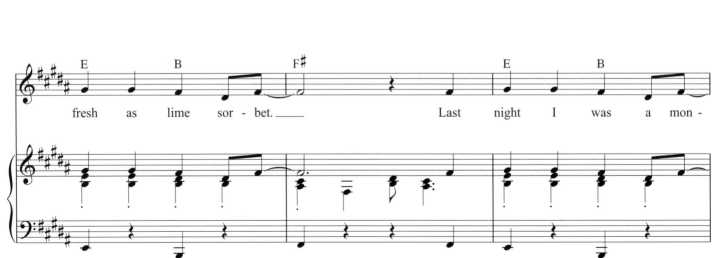

THIS PAGE HAS INTENTIONALLY BEEN LEFT BLANK TO FACILITATE PAGE TURNS.

IF THE WORLD SHOULD END

from *Spider-Man: Turn Off the Dark*

Music and Lyrics by Bono
and The Edge

MARY JANE WATSON: Don't think a- bout to- mor- row;_____ we've on- ly got to- day. There's noth- ing that I want from you,__ not a word__ you have to say. You are all I

THE DARK I KNOW WELL

from *Spring Awakening*

Music by Duncan Sheik
Lyrics by Steven Sater

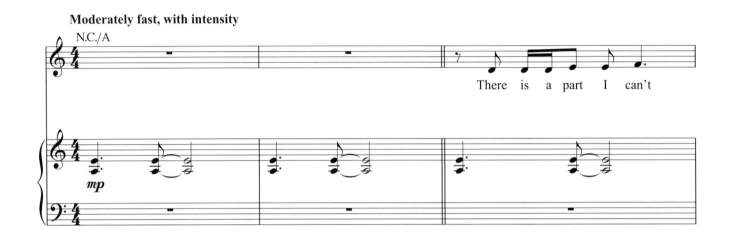

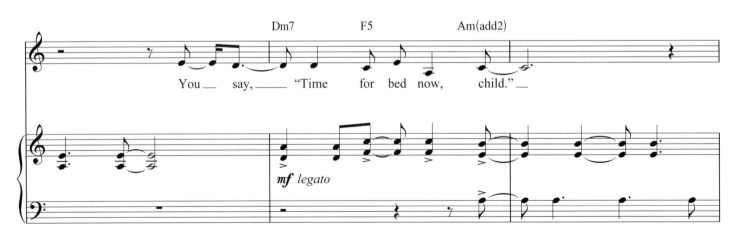

Sung by various characters (as indicated), the song can be sung as a solo.

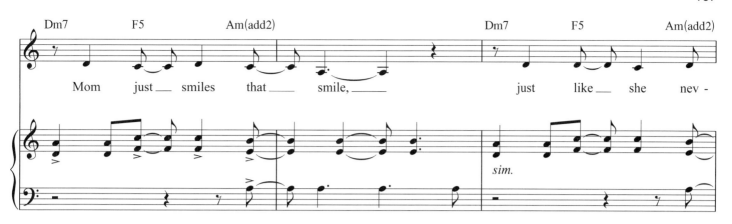

Mom just smiles that smile, just like she nev-

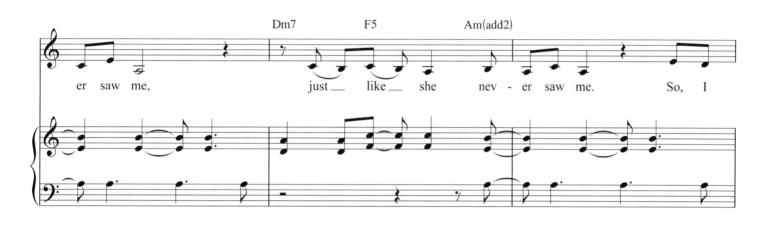

er saw me, just like she nev-er saw me. So, I

leave, want-in' just to hide, know-in' deep in-side

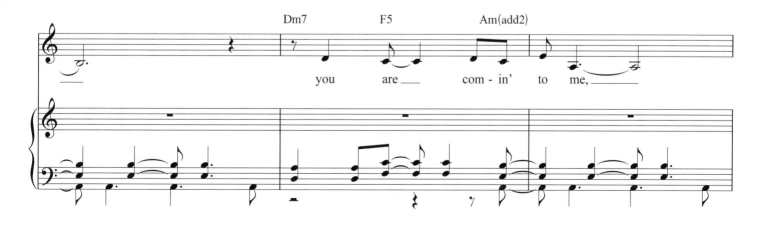

you are com-in' to me,

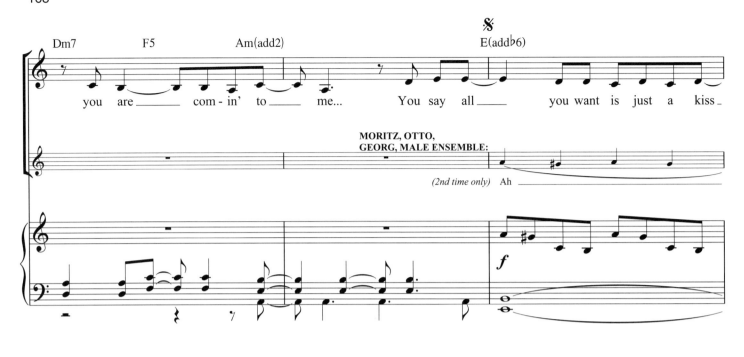

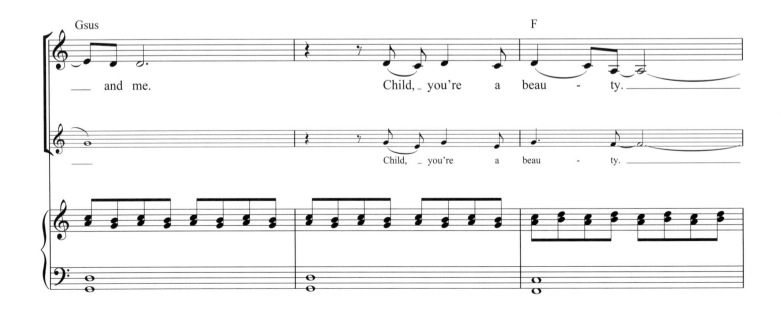

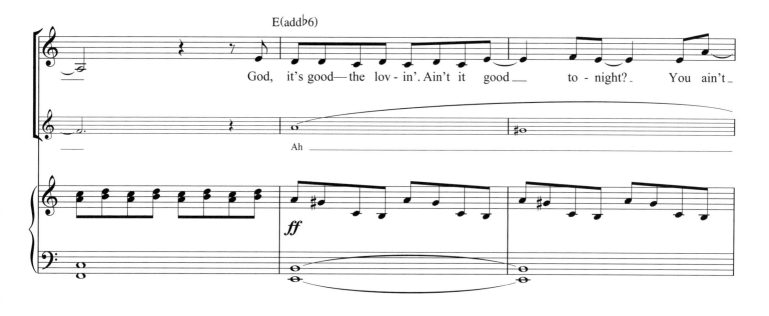

God, it's good—the lov-in'. Ain't it good __ to - night? __ You ain't __

Ah _____

__ seen noth-in' yet— gon - na {treat __ / teach __} you right. It's just you __ and me.

ah _____

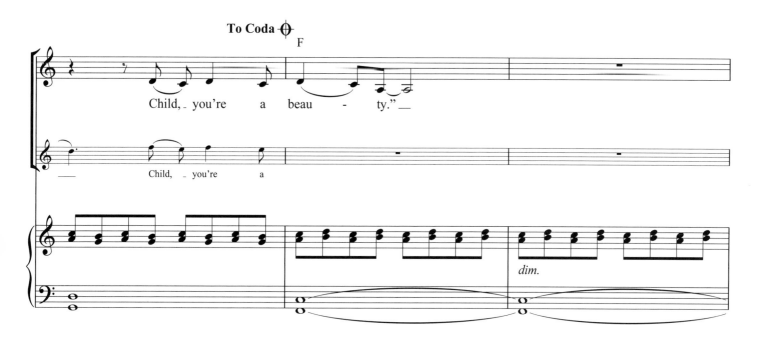

Child, __ you're a beau - ty." __

Child, __ you're a

dim.

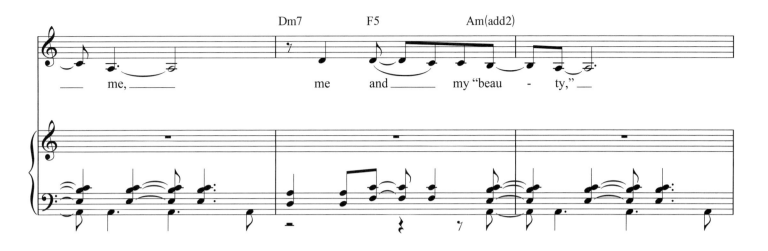

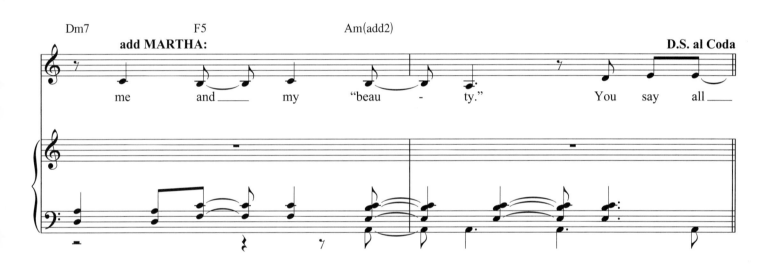

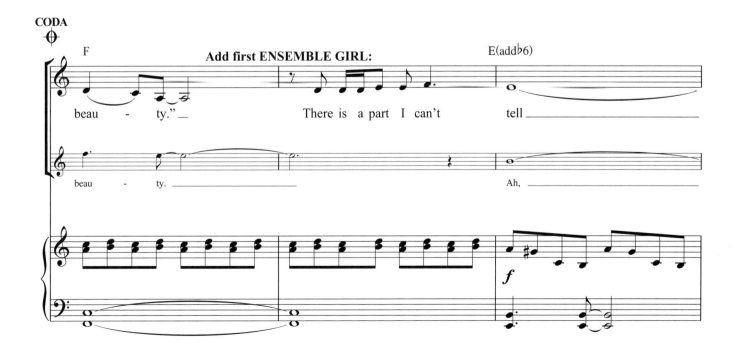

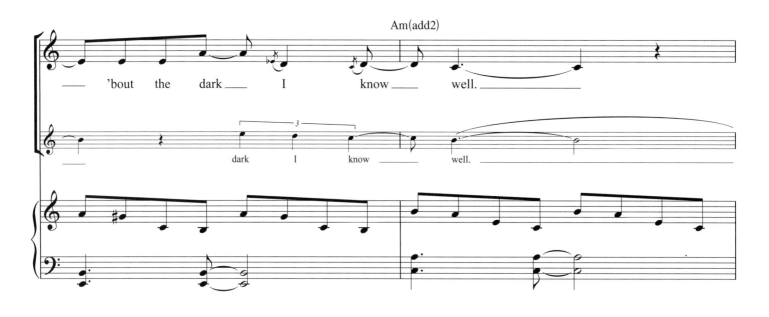

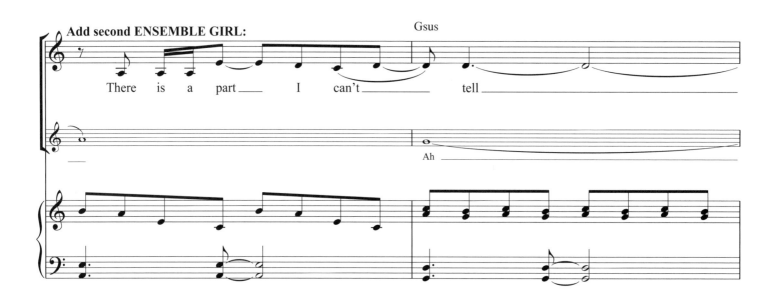

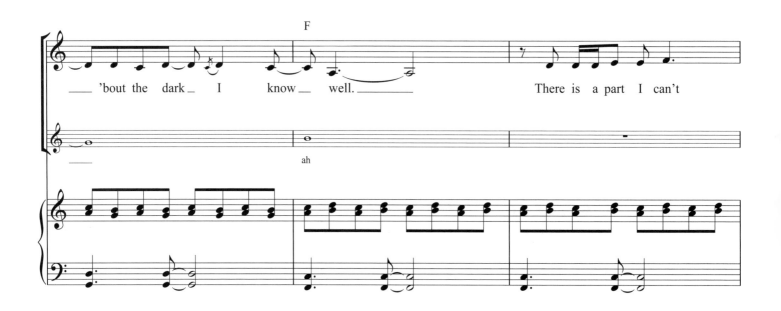

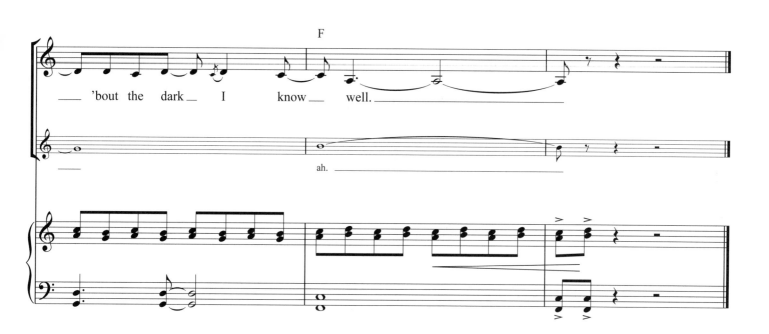

listen to
Lea Michelle

MAMA WHO BORE ME
from *Spring Awakening*

Music by Duncan Sheik
Lyrics by Steven Sater

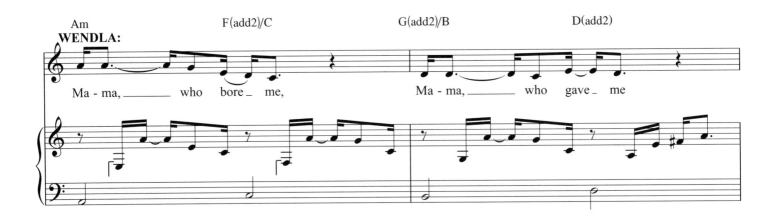

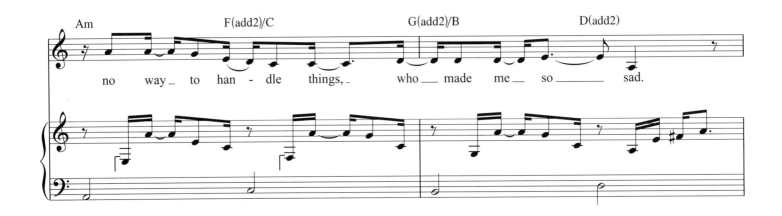

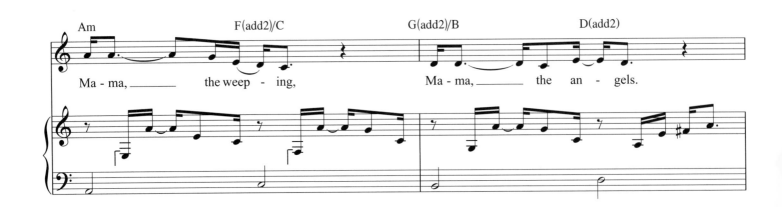

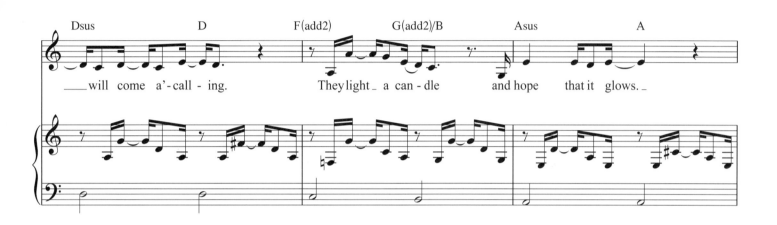

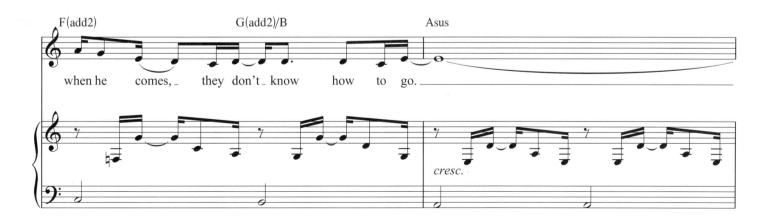

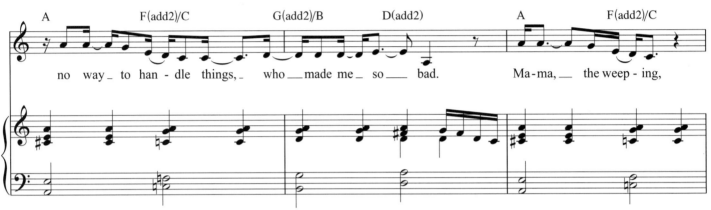

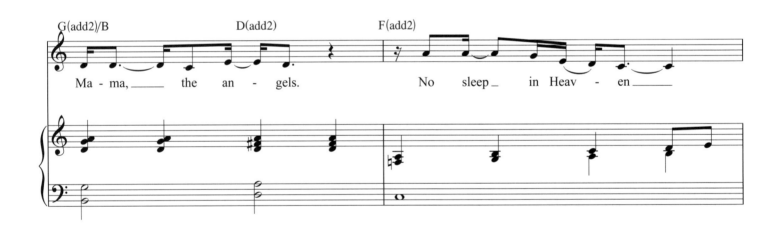

WHAT IT MEANS TO BE A FRIEND

from the Broadway Musical *13*

Music and Lyrics by
Jason Robert Brown

GIMME GIMME
from *Thoroughly Modern Millie*

Music by Jeanine Tesori
Lyrics by Dick Scanlan

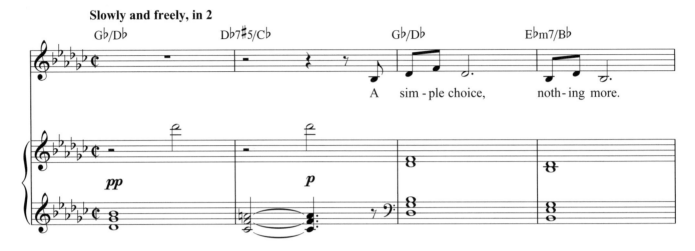

Slowly and freely, in 2

A sim-ple choice, noth-ing more.

Faster

This or that, ei-ther or. Mar-ry well, so-cial whirl, bus'-ness-man, clev-er girl, or

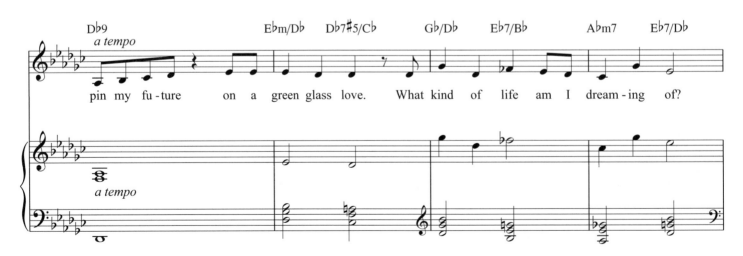

pin my fu-ture on a green glass love. What kind of life am I dream-ing of?

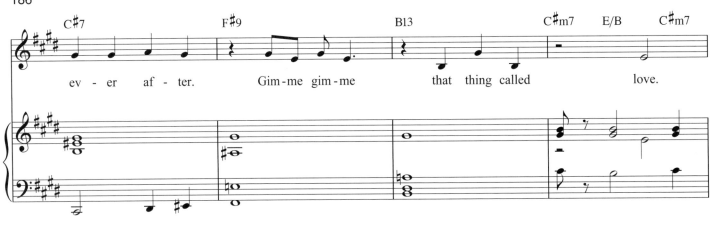

Moderately, with more confidence

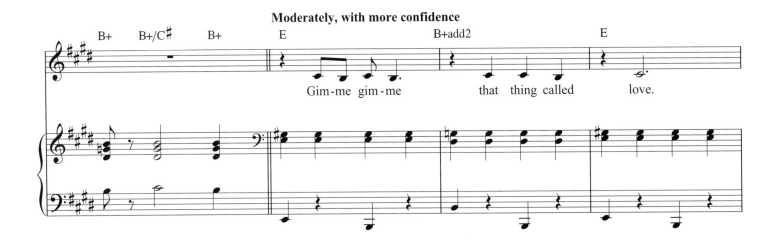

I'll want more time. Gim-me gim-me that thing called love. _____

Spirited, in 2

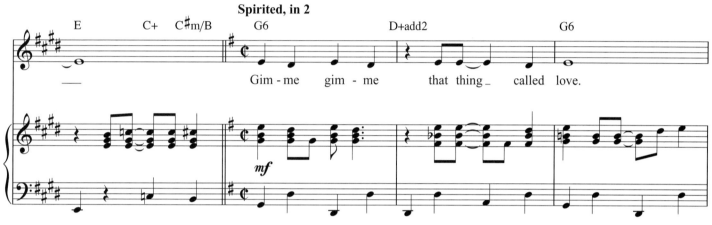

Gim - me gim - me that thing _ called love.

I'm free now. Gim-me gim-me that thing called love.

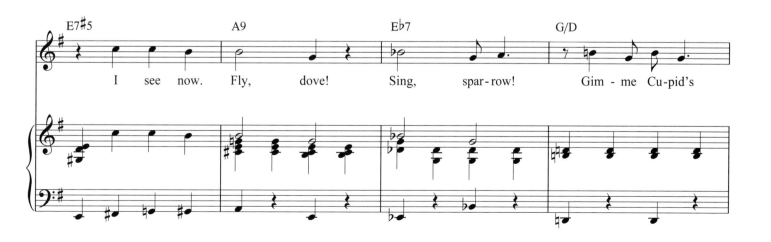

I see now. Fly, dove! Sing, spar-row! Gim - me Cu-pid's

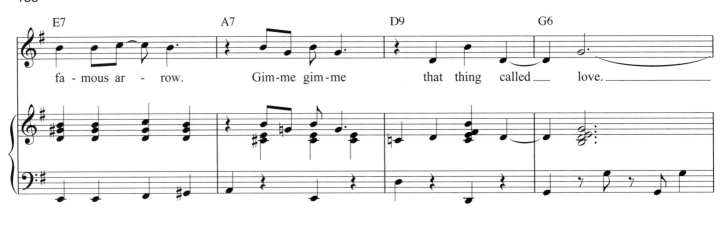

fa - mous ar - row. Gim-me gim-me that thing called __ love. ____

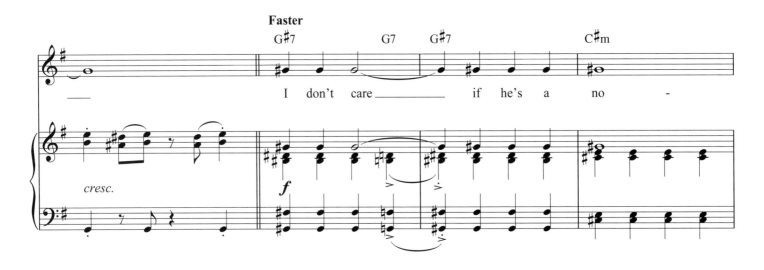

Faster

____ I don't care _____ if he's a no -

bod - y. ____ In my heart _____ he'll be a some -

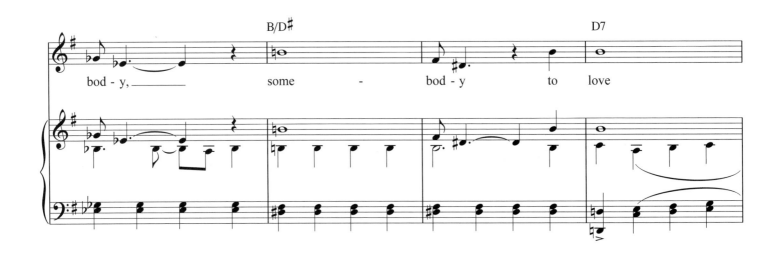

bod - y, _____ some - bod - y to love

NOT FOR THE LIFE OF ME

from *Thoroughly Modern Millie*

Music by Jeanine Tesori
Lyrics by Dick Scanlan

al - ways have this tic - ket in my poc - ket; a tic - ket home in my poc - ket to

Slower **Wide Swing - Hot Dixieland**

do with as I choose. Burn the bridge. _ Bet the store. _

Ba - by's com - in' home _ no more. _ Not for the life of

me. Break the lock. _ Post my bail.

* On the original cast recording there is a cut from here to **.

DEFYING GRAVITY
from the Broadway Musical *Wicked*

Music and Lyrics by
Stephen Schwartz

I'M NOT THAT GIRL
from the Broadway Musical *Wicked*

Music and Lyrics by
Stephen Schwartz

Sweet and steady, like a music box

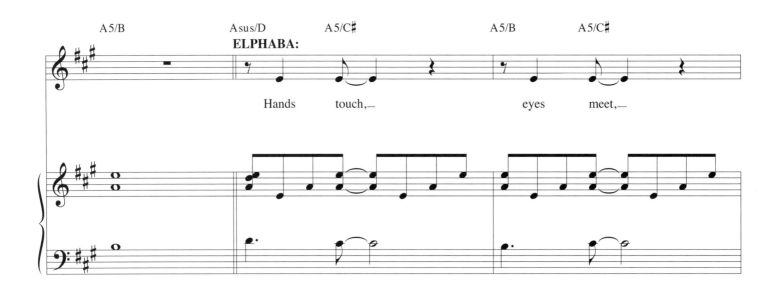

ELPHABA:
Hands touch,— eyes meet,—

Sud-den si - lence, sud-den heat.— Hearts leap— in a gid-dy

HOME
from the Broadway Musical *Wonderland*

Music by Frank Wildhorn
Lyrics by Jack Murphy